TABLE OF CONTENTS

About Jesse Tree 4

How to make a Jesse Tree 5

How to use these devotions 7

Dec. 1 - A little branch 8

Dec. 2 - A family resemblance 10

Dec. 3 - God's garden 12

Dec. 4 - A fresh start 14

Dec. 5 - A big move 16

Dec. 6 - A starry sky 18

Dec. 7 - A special son 20

Dec. 8 - Ten loving rules 22

Dec. 9 - A red rope 24

Dec. 10 - A loving rescuer 26

Dec. 11 - An underdog king 28

Dec. 12 - A shepherd-king 30

Dec. 13 - A living temple 32

Dec. 14 - A big risk 34

Dec. 15 - A bright light 36

Dec. 16 - A new parade 38

Dec. 17 - A dark fish belly 40

Dec. 18 - The best lion 42

Dec. 19 - A promise of peace 44

Dec. 20 - A long silence 46

Dec. 21 - A time to get ready 48

Dec. 22 - A new normal 50

Dec. 23 - A special request 52

Dec. 24 - A long journey 54

Dec. 25 - A birth announcement .. 56

Jesse Tree symbols 58

YOUR GUIDE TO CELEBRATING ADVENT

WITH JESSE TREE

The Jesse Tree tradition invites you to journey through the stories in Jesus's family tree to get ready to celebrate Christ's birth.

Each day of Advent, you read a Bible story about someone in Jesus's family tree and hang an ornament symbolizing the story on your Jesse Tree. As you decorate your tree, you see how God prepared for Jesus to be born through many generations. You remember that God's people waited a long time for Jesus to arrive. And in the stories of his ancestors, you hear echoes of his own life, death, and resurrection.

Jesse Tree gets its name from Isaiah 11:1: "A shoot shall come out from the stump of Jesse, and a branch shall grow out of his roots." Jesse was the father of David, Israel's greatest king. And Jesus is descended from the line of David. In fact, Jesus is the branch God promised would grow from Jesse's family tree. Each symbol represents a story from within this family tree and a step toward the birth of Jesus.

Go to www.faithward.org/jesse-tree to find everything you need for your journey through Advent with Jesse Tree.

HOW TO MAKE A JESSE TREE

Give a tree branch new life

Choose a tree branch without leaves, two to three feet high, that has a main branch with lots of smaller branches attached to it. Place the branch in a bucket of dirt or rocks and cover the bucket with green fabric, felt, or paper.

Fashion your tree from felt

Cut a tree with branches from brown felt. Glue it to a piece of green felt, 24" x 36." Glue on small wooden pegs to hang the ornaments. Or put Velcro® on the backs of the ornaments for attaching to the felt Jesse Tree.

Make a mobile

Make a mobile using a tree branch. Use fishing line to hang the branch from the ceiling. You'll need to make sure the symbols are balanced when you hang them on the branch so that the branch will remain level.

Just use a Christmas tree!

Repurpose or buy a small Christmas tree to use as your Jesse Tree. Or add the Jesse Tree ornaments to your Christmas tree, in a special space or right alongside your other ornaments.

HOW TO MAKE JESSE TREE ORNAMENTS

Use our templates for ornaments you can print at home:

1. **Go to** www.faithward.org/ornaments. Choose ornaments you can color yourself or pre-colored designs.

2. **Print the ornament patterns.** Standard settings for your printer should do the trick. You may want to use a heavier paper type like card stock to create a sturdier ornament.

3. **Color and decorate your ornaments.** Color in the ornaments with markers, crayons, and colored pencils. Or add dimension and texture with materials like fabric, colored paper, ribbons, sand, and foam.

4. **Prepare your ornaments for your tree.** Cut out your ornaments. Punch a hole at the top of each ornament and use ribbon or string to hang it on your tree. Or glue ornaments to blank wooden or foam circular ornaments from a craft store.

Go fully DIY with your ornaments

- Collect materials for your ornaments in the great outdoors! For example, you could use bark from a tree for the Jesse Tree symbol.

- Turn your recycling bin into craft supplies. For example, you could make a watchtower ornament with a toilet paper roll, or cut a crown out of a cardboard box.

- Put a twist on a classic. Fill or decorate clear, round ornaments to represent the Jesse Tree symbols.

- Use felt or fabric to create your ornaments. You could glue our ornament templates to fabric or sew your own symbols.

- Create origami ornaments. For example, make an origami star symbol.

- Make ornaments out of Legos or modeling clay.

HOW TO USE THESE DEVOTIONS WITH YOUR FAMILY

This devotional brings 25 Bible stories about the ancestors of Jesus to life for young readers. A symbol that you can turn into a Jesse Tree ornament accompanies each devotion. Go to www.faithward.org/ornaments to download and print ornament coloring pages depicting the symbols.

We imagined that an adult or an older child might read the Scripture passage and devotion aloud, while younger children color the day's picture. The devotions can be read daily from December 1 through December 25. Or, feel free to set your own pace and use them in the way that works best for your family.

If you'd like more context for a particular story, you can pull out your Bible and read the whole passage listed for that day, rather than the shorter selection included with the devotion. You can all ponder the "wonder" questions together. Wondering questions don't always have right or wrong answers. They are intended to help your family create lively discussion about the text.

This devotional was written with children elementary age and younger in mind. Teenagers and adults may prefer our personal Jesse Tree devotions, available for free at www.faithward.org/jesse-tree.

> **Access our complete guide to all-things Jesse Tree, including printable Jesse Tree ornaments kids can color, at www.faithward.org/jesse-tree.**

A LITTLE BRANCH

DECEMBER 1

READ: ISAIAH 11:1–2

A shoot shall come out from the stump of Jesse,

    and a branch shall grow out of his roots.

The spirit of the Lord shall rest on him,

    the spirit of wisdom and understanding,

    the spirit of counsel and might,

    the spirit of knowledge and the fear of the Lord.

LISTEN: Long ago, God's people were kicked out of their neighborhood and sent to live somewhere else. Life was hard, and their new neighbors were mean. God's people weren't being kind, either. It seemed like everyone only cared about themselves. Some little kids had no parents, and no one took care of them. Some old people had no family, and nobody bothered to check in on them.

God was fed up with that behavior. He cares about people and wants them to care about each other! So he told his people he was going to put a stop to it, just like you would cut down a big tree. Once that tree is cut down, that's the end. It stops growing.

But God made a promise: a tiny branch would sprout out of the dead tree stump. A fresh green shoot would start growing. Things wouldn't be dead anymore.

That little branch is Jesus. He's coming from the stump of his great-great-way-back-great-grandpa, Jesse. For the rest of Advent, we're going to hear more stories about the people in Jesus's family history and about how they helped God bring new life to his people.

WONDER: Have you ever seen a new shoot growing from an old tree? How does your heart feel when you see new plants growing in spring?

PRAY: God, you give us hope. Thank you for giving us Jesus, like new growth in spring. Would you help us to pay attention to him this Advent? Amen.

A FAMILY RESEMBLANCE

DECEMBER 2

READ: A SELECTION FROM GENESIS 1:26-31

Then God said, "Let us make humankind in our image, according to our likeness; and let them have dominion over the fish of the sea, and over the birds of the air, and over the cattle, and over all the wild animals of the earth, and over every creeping thing that creeps upon the earth."

So God created humankind in his image,

   in the image of God he created them;

   male and female he created them.

LISTEN: Did you know that when God made humans, he made us to look like him? God made all the stars and planets, all the beluga whales and blue jays, all the buffalo and begonias—but God didn't make any of those things in his image.

It was only when he made humans that he said, "Let's make them like us."

It's true! Something about you is made to look just like God.

Is it your eyes? When you smile, do they crinkle at the corners, just like God's do? Is it your hair? Does God have a cowlick in just the same place you do? Maybe it's your laugh. When something is so silly you can hardly breathe, do you sound like God sounds?

It's hard to know exactly what God looks and sounds like—except that we know what Jesus is like. Jesus is God in the form of a human being. Jesus looks exactly like God. He is God!

So if you're wondering what about you resembles God, you can just think about Jesus. You might not have his hair color, and your body might be built differently than his, but your heart can look just like Jesus's heart.

WONDER: What things about you—your personality or your character—are like Jesus? Can you think of ways that God made you to look like him?

> **PRAY:** Wow, God! We feel pretty special that you made us like you. Would you help us get to know Jesus so that we can look more and more like him? Amen.

GOD'S GARDEN

DECEMBER 3

READ: A SELECTION FROM GENESIS 3

So when the woman saw that the tree was good for food, and that it was a delight to the eyes, and that the tree was to be desired to make one wise, she took of its fruit and ate; and she also gave some to her husband, who was with her, and he ate. Then the eyes of both were opened, and they knew that they were naked; and they sewed fig leaves together and made loincloths for themselves. ...

Then the Lord God said, "See, the man has become like one of us, knowing good and evil; and now, he might reach out his hand and take also from the tree of life, and eat, and live forever"— therefore the Lord God sent him forth from the garden of Eden, to till the ground from which he was taken.

LISTEN:
Sunshine warms the garden, and big trees make cool, shady spots in just the right places. Flowers bloom wildly. Birds sing. Bunnies scamper. This garden, with a tree right in the middle, is the place where God lives with the people he created.

But when Adam and Eve ate the fruit, God knew he couldn't trust them to live in the garden any more. He sent them away. Since then, people haven't been able to live as close to God as Adam and Eve did.

The good news is that God has been working hard so that we can live with him again. In the Bible, we get a sneak preview of the end of the story. God is building a city—with a tree right in the middle—where we will live with him again!

So how do we get from the tree at the beginning to the tree at the end? God uses another tree. That tree got chopped down and put together in the shape of a cross. When Jesus died on that tree, he closed the distance between us and God. Jesus made it so that we could return to joyful, peaceful life with God.

WONDER:
What things do you do that make you feel far from God? What do you look forward to about living near to God?

> **PRAY:** Loving God, we're sorry for doing things that put a gap between us and you. Jesus, thank you for closing that gap when you died. We're excited to live with you in the city with a tree! Amen.

A FRESH START

DECEMBER 4

READ: A SELECTION FROM GENESIS 6:11-9:13

The flood continued forty days on the earth; and the waters increased, and bore up the ark, and it rose high above the earth. The waters swelled and increased greatly on the earth; and the ark floated on the face of the waters. The waters swelled so mightily on the earth that all the high mountains under the whole heaven were covered; the waters swelled above the mountains, covering them fifteen cubits deep. And all flesh died that moved on the earth, birds, domestic animals, wild animals, all swarming creatures that swarm on the earth, and all human beings; everything on dry land in whose nostrils was the breath of life died.

LISTEN: When God created Adam, he squatted down on the ground, took a bunch of dirt and mud, packed it together, and made it into the shape of a man. Then God leaned over it and breathed God's own breath into Adam's nose, and Adam came to life. He lived because he had the breath of life in him.

Now, in this story, God takes the breath of life away.

Everyone in the whole world was doing terrible things, and it broke God's heart. When God breathed life into Adam, he expected Adam and all the people after him to love each other and care for each other and to respect and love God. But it didn't take long for people to start hating each other and hurting each other and not loving God, either.

It got to be so bad that God decided just to end it. So he flooded everything so that every animal and every person died, except Noah, his family, and some animals.

The very same breath that he breathed into Adam, God took away from everyone. God wanted to start fresh. And he did—God has given us a new kind of breath, Holy Spirit breath.

In a way, God has breathed into us just like he breathed into Adam. We live because we have the Holy Spirit, the breath of life, in us.

WONDER: How does it feel to take a deep breath of fresh air? What does Holy Spirit breath feel like inside you?

PRAY: God, you give the breath of life and you take it away. Would you fill us with your Holy Spirit so that we can live in a way that shows our love for you and our love for other people? Amen.

A BIG MOVE

DECEMBER 5

READ: A SELECTION FROM GENESIS 12:1–7

Now the Lord said to Abram, "Go from your country and your kindred and your father's house to the land that I will show you. I will make of you a great nation, and I will bless you, and make your name great, so that you will be a blessing. I will bless those who bless you, and the one who curses you I will curse; and in you all the families of the earth shall be blessed."

LISTEN: Abraham and Sarah packed up all their things. They said goodbye to their friends. They visited their favorite restaurant one more time. They took one last walk through their neighborhood. And then they loaded everything up and moved far, far away because God asked them to.

God told them that if they moved to this new place, God would use them to show his love to a lot more people. Abraham and Sarah were nervous about moving to a new place, but they were excited that God was going to use them to show his love.

Jesus also knows those feelings. He knows what it's like to leave behind things that are familiar and go someplace new.

Before Jesus came to earth as a little baby, he lived in heaven with God. It's very comfortable there—never too cold, never too hot. You always feel full of joy, and you're never grumpy. But Jesus knew that if he came to earth, he could show God's love to a lot more people. Because Jesus left that comfortable place, he gave us the chance to know God's love.

WONDER: What does it feel like to go somewhere new? Why was Jesus willing to leave heaven to show God's love to us?

> **PRAY:** Jesus, thank you so much for coming to earth so we can be loved by God. Will you help me do hard things sometimes so other people can know your love, too? Amen.

A STARRY SKY

DECEMBER 6

READ: A SELECTION FROM GENESIS 15:1–6

[God] brought [Abraham] outside and said, "Look toward heaven and count the stars, if you are able to count them." Then he said to him, "So shall your descendants be." And he believed the Lord; and the Lord reckoned it to him as righteousness.

LISTEN: If there's a clear night this week, go outside with your family before you go to bed. (If you live somewhere cold, bundle up!) Find a spot where you can see the sky and look up. Hopefully, the sky is dark enough that you're able to see the tiny pinpricks of stars, way off in the distance. The longer you look, the more stars you'll be able to see.

This is how God showed Abraham how big Abraham's family would be. God promised that Abraham would have one son and so many grandchildren and great-grandchildren that he wouldn't be able to count them, even if he tried.

Did you realize that you are part of Abraham's family? When God showed Abraham all those stars, he was including you, too! Because of Jesus Christ, we are adopted into that same family—the family of Abraham and the family of God. The people in the stories you're reading this Advent are your great-great-great grandmas and grandpas!

WONDER: Do you think Abraham tried to count all the stars he could see? What does it feel like to be part of God's family?

> **PRAY:** God of Abraham, Isaac, and Jacob, thank you for making me part of your family. I'm thankful that I get to be in the same family as Jesus. Amen.

A SPECIAL SON

DECEMBER 7

READ: A SELECTION FROM GENESIS 37:1–36

Now [Jacob] loved Joseph more than any other of his children, because he was the son of his old age; and he had made him a long robe with sleeves. But when his brothers saw that their father loved him more than all his brothers, they hated him, and could not speak peaceably to him. … So when Joseph came to his brothers, they stripped him of his robe, the long robe with sleeves that he wore; and they took him and threw him into a pit. The pit was empty; there was no water in it.

LISTEN: Little brothers can be hard to get along with. In Joseph's case, his father, Jacob, loved him more than all his brothers. Jacob gave Joseph a special coat, which made them jealous. And at the breakfast table in the mornings, Joseph liked to tell his family about his dreams. He often dreamed about being in charge of all his brothers. That made his brothers furious.

Big brothers can be tough to deal with, too. In this story, Joseph's jealous brothers decided to kill him and his crazy dreams. They didn't quite kill him, but they did take his special coat and sell him to some slave traders for twenty pieces of silver.

Joseph isn't the only child to have been his father's favorite and make his brothers want to kill him. The Bible says that Jesus is God's beloved son, kind of like God's favorite. And when Jesus started sharing his message with people, they got so mad they tried to kill him. They took his coat, too.

The good news is that the story about Joseph and his brothers ends well. Joseph does end up being in charge, but it helps save his family—just like in the story of Jesus. Jesus is sold for thirty pieces of silver and then killed. But he comes back to life and is king over the whole world. The people that hated Jesus are the same people that he came to save. And do you know who those people are? They are you and me.

WONDER: How did Joseph's brothers feel? How could Joseph still love his brothers when they hated him so much?

> **PRAY:** Wow, Jesus! I'm amazed that you and Joseph were willing to love the people who hated you. I'm also thankful because it means that you love me and have saved me. Amen.

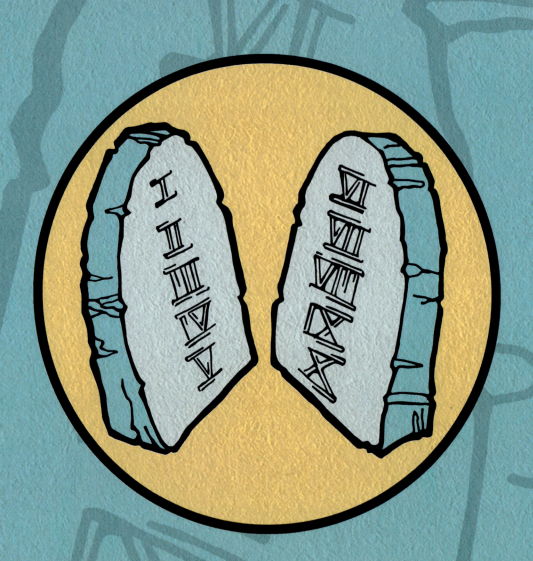

TEN LOVING RULES

DECEMBER 8

READ: A SELECTION FROM DEUTERONOMY 5:1–22

Moses convened all Israel, and said to them: "Hear, O Israel, the statutes and ordinances that I am addressing to you today; you shall learn them and observe them diligently. The Lord our God made a covenant with us at Horeb. Not with our ancestors did the Lord make this covenant, but with us, who are all of us here alive today. The Lord spoke with you face to face at the mountain, out of the fire."

LISTEN: Have you ever seen the list of rules at the pool?

> Shower first.
>
> No running.
>
> No diving.
>
> No unsupervised children.
>
> No food or drinks.

Who made up those rules? Showering first just seems silly, doesn't it? It's like the pool people are trying to spoil all our fun!

The Ten Commandments can seem that way, too, like a list of rules that God gave us to ruin our fun. But God's not like that. He gave the Israelites the Ten Commandments to help everyone live together well and to set them apart as his people. He didn't tack up the Ten Commandments on a wall and leave the Israelites on their own. No, God had already chosen the people of Israel and promised to love them. When he gave the commandments to Moses, he planned to stay with his people and keep loving them.

We should follow God's commandments not just because they'll keep us safe, like the rules at the pool. We should follow them because God loves us. And the best news of all is that Jesus helps us to follow them!

WONDER: Which of the Ten Commandments is hardest for you to follow? Is there a commandment you think is most important?

> **PRAY:** God, will you remind me of how much you already love me? Help me remember that following your rules doesn't make you love me. Amen.

A RED ROPE

DECEMBER 9

READ: A SELECTION FROM JOSHUA 2:1–21

The king of Jericho sent orders to Rahab, "Bring out the men who have come to you, who entered your house." But the woman took the two men and hid them. ...

She came up to them on the roof and said to the men, "I know that the Lord has given you the land ... The Lord your God is indeed God in heaven above and on earth below. Now then, since I have dealt kindly with you, swear to me by the Lord that you in turn will deal kindly with my family." ... The men said to her, "Our life for yours! If you do not tell this business of ours, then we will deal kindly and faithfully with you when the Lord gives us the land. ...

"Tie this crimson cord in the window. ... If a hand is laid upon any who are with you in the house, we shall bear the responsibility for their death." ... She tied the crimson cord in the window.

LISTEN: The Israelites have been wandering in the desert for 40 years, and now it's finally time to move into the land that God promised them. That land is called Canaan, and it's filled with people who don't love or trust God.

But when two Israelite spies sneak into the city of Jericho in Canaan, they get help from someone they least expect: a woman named Rahab. Even though she's not an Israelite, she has heard about the God of Israel. And she believes that he is the true God. After she helps the Israelite spies, she asks them to protect her family when the Israelite army comes to knock down Jericho. The spies agree—if she hangs a red rope in her window so they know which house to protect. The red rope will save Rahab's life.

That red rope hanging in her window looks a lot like a trail of blood, which reminds us of the blood of Jesus. When Jesus died, his blood saved our lives, just like the red rope saved Rahab's life. If we trust in God, like Rahab did, we get to join God's family and be protected.

WONDER: Why didn't the Israelite spies tell Rahab to hang a purple rope in her window? Do you think Rahab was afraid to help the Israelite spies?

> **PRAY:** Jesus, thank you for bleeding so that I can live.
> I'm glad I can be part of your family. Amen.

A LOVING RESCUER

DECEMBER 10

READ: A SELECTION FROM RUTH 3:1-4:12

Naomi her mother-in-law said to her, "My daughter, I need to seek some security for you, so that it may be well with you. Now here is our kinsman Boaz, with whose young women you have been working. See, he is winnowing barley tonight at the threshing floor. Now wash and anoint yourself, and put on your best clothes and go down to the threshing floor; but do not make yourself known to the man until he has finished eating and drinking. When he lies down, observe the place where he lies; then, go and uncover his feet and lie down; and he will tell you what to do." [Ruth] said to her, "All that you tell me I will do."

LISTEN: In Israel, there were rules to protect widows, women whose husbands had died. Back then, women didn't have jobs, so they couldn't make money to pay for food or a house. And men were the ones to carry on the family name, so if a woman had no sons, the family would end with her.

So there was a special rule to protect a widow with no sons. The rule was that the brother of the widow's dead husband had to marry the widow. (Back then, it was sometimes okay to have more than one wife.) That brother was called the "kinsman redeemer." Kinsman means a relative, and redeemer means someone who rescues you. The brother would rescue the widow and her family by paying for food, giving them a place to live, and carrying on the family name.

In this story, Boaz is the kinsman redeemer for Ruth and Naomi. Naomi's husband and Ruth's husband both died, and Naomi and Ruth were helpless without any sons. But they weren't hopeless. Boaz stepped up to marry Ruth so that the family could continue.

Much later in the Bible, we read about another kinsman redeemer. That kinsman redeemer is Jesus. Everyone in the world is as helpless as Ruth and Naomi were. But the Bible says Jesus is like the groom at a wedding, and the church is his bride. Like Boaz, he steps up to marry us, to join his life with ours and rescue us.

WONDER: What about Boaz made him willing to marry Ruth, even though he didn't know her? Why do you think Jesus was willing to rescue us?

> **PRAY:** Jesus, thanks for taking me and making me part of the wonderful family of God. Amen.

AN UNDERDOG KING

DECEMBER 11

READ: A SELECTION FROM 1 SAMUEL 16:1–15

The Lord said to Samuel, "How long will you grieve over Saul? I have rejected him from being king over Israel. Fill your horn with oil and set out; I will send you to Jesse the Bethlehemite, for I have provided for myself a king among his sons." …

Jesse made seven of his sons pass before Samuel, and Samuel said to Jesse, "The Lord has not chosen any of these." Samuel said to Jesse, "Are all your sons here?" And he said, "There remains yet the youngest, but he is keeping the sheep." … He sent and brought [David] in. Now he was ruddy, and had beautiful eyes, and was handsome. The Lord said, "Rise and anoint him; for this is the one." Then Samuel took the horn of oil, and anointed him.

LISTEN: God *loves* to make the underdog the hero of the story. God doesn't usually pick the strongest person or the coolest one or the oldest one. He likes to use weak, dorky, little siblings.

If you looked at him, you wouldn't think David would make a very good king. He didn't know how to fight in battles. He had never worked in city government. He had spent a lot of time with sheep, and that was about it.

But that's exactly the person God wanted to use. The little brother. It's kind of like how God picked the people of Israel—a tiny group of people who weren't very strong or impressive on their own—to be the people he would bless the whole world through.

And it's a lot like how God decided to show his love to everyone by coming as a tiny, fragile baby. If you looked at Jesus, you wouldn't think he would make a very good king. When he was a kid, he spent a lot of time building chairs with his dad. When he grew up, he didn't show everyone how cool and powerful he was. He allowed the government to kill him.

In Jesus, God makes himself the underdog so that we can live.

WONDER: What other stories have an underdog as the hero? How is God using you, even though you're not a grown-up or the most powerful and richest person?

> **PRAY:** Sometimes you surprise me, God! You like to use people whom the world doesn't think are important. Help me remember that you want to use me, too. Amen.

A SHEPHERD-KING

DECEMBER 12

READ: A SELECTION FROM 2 SAMUEL 5:1–5

The Lord said to [David]: "It is you who shall be shepherd of my people Israel, you who shall be ruler over Israel." So all the elders of Israel came to the king at Hebron; and King David made a covenant with them at Hebron before the Lord, and they anointed David king over Israel.

LISTEN: Kings and shepherds seem like exact opposites. Kings sit on thrones. They wear expensive clothes and talk to important people. Shepherds, on the other hand, stand on the hillsides. They wear clothes that can get dirty, and they talk mostly to sheep.

David was both. He was a shepherd that God chose to be king. A shepherd would probably make a very good king, since shepherds have to be humble and they probably care more about people than about power.

Can you guess who else is a shepherd-king?

If you guessed Jesus, you're exactly right. Jesus is the Good Shepherd. He knows all of us as well as a shepherd knows his sheep, and he was willing to die so that we can live. Jesus is also the King of kings. He beat the powers of sin and death. Now he sits on his throne, ruling over all of creation.

WONDER: Why would a shepherd be a good king?

> **PRAY:** King Jesus, thank you for having the heart of a shepherd! Would you help the leaders of our cities and nations be as kind and gentle as shepherds, too? Amen.

A LIVING TEMPLE

DECEMBER 13

READ: A SELECTION FROM 1 KINGS 5–6

So I intend to build a house for the name of the Lord my God, as the Lord said to my father David, "Your son, whom I will set on your throne in your place, shall build the house for my name." ...

Now the word of the Lord came to Solomon, "Concerning this house that you are building, if you will walk in my statutes, obey my ordinances, and keep all my commandments by walking in them, then I will establish my promise with you, which I made to your father David. I will dwell among the children of Israel, and will not forsake my people Israel."

So Solomon built the house, and finished it.

LISTEN: The temple was *really* important. (If you read all of 1 Kings 6, you'll see how intricate and beautiful it was! It was very tall, and the whole thing was made of gorgeous wood, with pictures of trees and fruit and angels carved into it. The inside was covered in gold, so everything gleamed and sparkled.)

It wasn't just a building. It was the place where God and humans could meet. Before Solomon built the temple, God met his people in a big tent called a tabernacle.

Inside the temple, there was a special room, called the Holy of Holies, where God lived. In that place, God and humans could be together.

But God had even better plans. He didn't want people to have to go into a tiny room to be with him in person. (And not just anyone—only certain people—could go into the room.)

So God decided that he would become the temple. Jesus called himself the temple. He is both God and human, the place where the two meet. We don't have to go into a special room anymore. Now we can know God directly because of Jesus!

WONDER: Why did God decide to let us meet him anywhere, not just in a special room in the temple?

> **PRAY:** Jesus, thank you for being the temple, the place where I can meet God. By your Holy Spirit, I am connected with God. Help me sense you with me today. Amen.

A BIG RISK

DECEMBER 14

READ: A SELECTION FROM ESTHER 4

When they told Mordecai what Esther had said, Mordecai told them to reply to Esther, "Do not think that in the king's palace you will escape any more than all the other Jews. For if you keep silence at such a time as this, relief and deliverance will rise for the Jews from another quarter, but you and your father's family will perish. Who knows? Perhaps you have come to royal dignity for just such a time as this." Then Esther said in reply to Mordecai, "Go, gather all the Jews to be found in Susa, and hold a fast on my behalf, and neither eat nor drink for three days, night or day. I and my maids will also fast as you do. After that I will go to the king, though it is against the law; and if I perish, I perish."

LISTEN: King Ahasuerus just agreed to order all the Jews to be killed. So Queen Esther decided that she would try to talk him out of it. It might mean that she would be killed, too, since no one was allowed to talk to the king without being invited.

She was willing to die to save her people.

Does that sound familiar? Jesus was also willing to die to save his people. And he wasn't just willing to die. He actually died, and his death brought us life. Jesus took the biggest risk of all, which frees us to take risks, too.

Death isn't so scary anymore when we remember that Jesus has already died and beat death.

Esther's life belonged to Jesus, so she was free to risk her life. By taking that risk, she brought life for her people. The risks we take might also bring life to other people!

WONDER: What hard or scary things can you do that can help make other people's lives better?

> **PRAY:** Jesus Christ, thank you for making death less scary. Help me be brave so I can help other people. Amen.

A BRIGHT LIGHT

DECEMBER 15

READ: A SELECTION FROM ISAIAH 9:2–7

The people who walked in darkness

  have seen a great light;

those who lived in a land of deep darkness—

  on them light has shined.

LISTEN: Have you ever been in a place where it's pitch black? If you've ever gone camping, maybe you know the feeling of not being able to see anything. You're in the woods at night, and you can't see the moon or stars. You can't see anything at all.

Or maybe it's just really dark in your bedroom at night. That can feel scary and confusing, can't it? When you don't know what's around you, you might feel afraid and lonely and not want to move.

This is the kind of deep darkness the people of Israel walked in. Well, it wasn't actually nighttime all the time, but it had started to feel that way. They couldn't see the person who was coming to save them. After a while, they started to think he might never come. They had no hope.

This chapter in Isaiah reminds the people of Israel of the light that is coming. The sun will come up in the morning! It won't be nighttime forever.

The light that is coming is a person, and his name is Jesus. He is coming to save his people. When he is here, we don't have to be scared or sad anymore. We can feel full of peace and joy.

Jesus is the light of the world. From now until Christmas, we are getting ready to have the night become day. Jesus is on his way!

WONDER: How do you feel when it's completely dark? What about during the day, when it's bright?

> **PRAY:** God of light, I can't wait for you to come. Would You turn the world's darkness into light? Amen.

A NEW PARADE

DECEMBER 16

READ: ISAIAH 11:6–8

The wolf shall live with the lamb,
   the leopard shall lie down with the kid,
the calf and the lion and the fatling together,
   and a little child shall lead them.
The cow and the bear shall graze,
   their young shall lie down together;
   and the lion shall eat straw like the ox.
The nursing child shall play over the hole of the asp,
   and the weaned child shall put its hand on the adder's den.

LISTEN: This scene reminds me of a silly parade! A wolf walks next to a lamb. A baby cow and a bear and a lion march in a line, led by a child. Halfway through, the child stops to play with a snake. And on the edge of the street, a leopard and a baby goat sit on their picnic blanket to watch.

Can you imagine a parade like that? If you've ever been to the zoo, you know those animals can't be together. The wolf would eat the lamb! The bear and the lion would attack the cow. The snake would bite the child. The leopard would gobble up the goat. It would be the worst parade ever!

But this is the world God imagines. God is creating a world where that parade is just an average Monday. Predators and prey will get along. Instead of fighting, we'll work together and play together.

That's the world where Jesus Christ is king.

WONDER: When all the animals get along, which one do you want to play with?

PRAY: God, I'm excited for the day when we can have a parade with lions and bears. I pray that your kingdom would come soon! Amen.

A DARK FISH BELLY

DECEMBER 17

READ: JONAH 3:1–5

The word of the Lord came to Jonah a second time, saying, "Get up, go to Nineveh, that great city, and proclaim to it the message that I tell you." So Jonah set out and went to Nineveh, according to the word of the Lord. Now Nineveh was an exceedingly large city, a three days' walk across. Jonah began to go into the city, going a day's walk. And he cried out, "Forty days more, and Nineveh shall be overthrown!" And the people of Nineveh believed God; they proclaimed a fast, and everyone, great and small, put on sackcloth.

LISTEN: Jonah was not a very good listener. Or actually, maybe he could hear just fine, but he wasn't so great at obeying. When God told him to go to Nineveh, he hopped on the first boat in the other direction!

God *loved* the people of Nineveh and wanted them to know him, so he stirred up a big storm to get Jonah's attention. Jonah asked the sailors to throw him off the ship to get the storm to stop, which they did. And then a giant fish came along and gulped him down. Jonah stayed in that fish's belly for three days.

When the fish spit him back out, Jonah decided to obey God and go to Nineveh. He arrived in Nineveh, told the people God's message, and they believed!

Jonah wasn't the only person to hang out in a dark, damp place for three days. That's what Jesus did while he was in the tomb. Jesus was much more willing to obey than Jonah was, and Jesus's obedience also meant that lots of people had the chance to trust God!

WONDER: Why do you think the people of Nineveh believed God?

> **PRAY:** God, help me to obey you so that other people can know you. What things do you want me to do to follow you? Amen.

THE BEST LION

DECEMBER 18

READ: A SELECTION FROM DANIEL 6

The conspirators came and found Daniel praying and seeking mercy before his God. Then they approached the king and said concerning the interdict, "O king! Did you not sign an interdict, that anyone who prays to anyone, divine or human, within thirty days except to you, O king, shall be thrown into a den of lions?" ...

Then the king gave the command, and Daniel was brought and thrown into the den of lions. The king said to Daniel, "May your God, whom you faithfully serve, deliver you!" ...

Then, at break of day, the king got up and hurried to the den of lions. When he came near the den where Daniel was, he cried out anxiously to Daniel, "O Daniel, servant of the living God, has your God whom you faithfully serve been able to deliver you from the lions?" Daniel then said to the king, "O king, live forever! My God sent his angel and shut the lions' mouths so that they would not hurt me, because I was found blameless before him; and also before you, O king, I have done no wrong."

LISTEN: Daniel was brave. The reason he was brave was because he trusted God. Daniel knew that God was powerful and would take care of him.

Daniel wasn't scared to pray to God, even though the king had made a rule that people could only pray to the king. Daniel wasn't scared to go into the lions' den, even though the lions were hungry and ready to eat him. Daniel knew that God would take care of him.

And God did! God sent an angel to shut the lions' mouths so they couldn't bite Daniel.

Did you know that when God sends an angel, it's almost like he sends himself? Angels are not just God's friends. They represent God. So the angel in the den with Daniel was almost like God in the den with Daniel.

God himself was protecting Daniel! God—the Lion of Judah—showed the lions of Babylon that he was more powerful and that he would protect Daniel.

WONDER: When is a time that God helped you feel brave? What is it like to feel God's presence with you?

> **PRAY:** God, thank you for being powerful and protecting me. Would you help me trust you? Amen.

A PROMISE OF PEACE

DECEMBER 19

READ: A SELECTION FROM MICAH 5:1–5

But you, O Bethlehem of Ephrathah,

who are one of the little clans of Judah,

from you shall come forth for me

one who is to rule in Israel,

… And he shall stand and feed his flock in the strength of the Lord,

in the majesty of the name of the Lord his God.

And they shall live secure, for now he shall be great

to the ends of the earth;

and he shall be the one of peace.

LISTEN: Do you know what a prophecy is? It's kind of like a promise about the future. A prophecy tells us what's going to happen.

When someone tells you something that's going to happen, do you usually believe it? Maybe you believe it if your dad says he'll pick you up from school, but not if your sister says she'll let you play with her toy. It depends on who is making the promise!

When God or his prophets say something, it will definitely happen. So when God's prophet Micah says that someone is coming who will rule Israel, he really means it. A king is coming who will stand and feed his flock—he'll take care of his people. And he will bring peace everywhere he goes.

Micah prophesied that many, many years ago. But Jesus really came! He cared for his people and was full of peace.

We can be confident that Jesus will come again and his peaceful kingdom will stay forever. He is the Prince of Peace.

WONDER: How does it feel when a promise is broken? Why can we trust God's promises?

PRAY: Prince of Peace, you are a good and loving king. I can't wait for you to come back. Amen.

A LONG SILENCE

DECEMBER 20

READ: A SELECTION FROM LUKE 1:5–25

Then there appeared to him an angel of the Lord, standing at the right side of the altar of incense. When Zechariah saw him, he was terrified; and fear overwhelmed him. But the angel said to him, "Do not be afraid, Zechariah, for your prayer has been heard. Your wife Elizabeth will bear you a son, and you will name him John. … He will turn many of the people of Israel to the Lord their God. With the spirit and power of Elijah he will go before him, to turn the hearts of parents to their children, and the disobedient to the wisdom of the righteous, to make ready a people prepared for the Lord." Zechariah said to the angel, "How will I know that this is so? For I am an old man, and my wife is getting on in years." The angel replied, "I am Gabriel. I stand in the presence of God, and I have been sent to speak to you and to bring you this good news. But now, because you did not believe my words, which will be fulfilled in their time, you will become mute, unable to speak, until the day these things occur."

LISTEN: Is it hard or easy for you to stay quiet for a long time? For most of us, it's pretty hard. There are so many things to talk about!

But Zechariah didn't have a choice. God made him unable to speak for about nine months, while his wife, Elizabeth, was pregnant with their son. He couldn't talk to Elizabeth about what things they needed to get ready for a baby. He couldn't tell her that she made a delicious dinner. He couldn't talk to his friends about his job.

I wonder if being forced to be silent was actually very helpful for Zechariah. Sometimes, when we're so busy chatting, we don't notice God's quiet presence. Maybe not talking helped Zechariah see God with him during the day.

I wonder if it would be helpful for us to have some quiet moments during Advent. If we never turn off the Christmas music, we might drown out God's voice.

God is with you right now, and if you're quiet, you might notice him!

WONDER: If you were Zechariah, what things would you want to say? Where do you notice God today?

> **PRAY:** God, I'm calming down and trying to listen to you. What do you want to tell me? Amen.

A TIME TO GET READY

DECEMBER 21

READ: MATTHEW 3:1–6

In those days John the Baptist appeared in the wilderness of Judea, proclaiming, "Repent, for the kingdom of heaven has come near." This is the one of whom the prophet Isaiah spoke when he said,

"The voice of one crying out in the wilderness:

'Prepare the way of the Lord,

make his paths straight.'"

Now John wore clothing of camel's hair with a leather belt around his waist, and his food was locusts and wild honey. Then the people of Jerusalem and all Judea were going out to him, and all the region along the Jordan, and they were baptized by him in the river Jordan, confessing their sins.

LISTEN: When someone comes to your house, they don't just come right in. They usually knock or ring the doorbell. It's how they announce that they're coming.

If your mom or dad is especially tidy, they might pick up a few toys and stack a few papers before they answer the door. The time between hearing the doorbell and answering the door gives them a chance to clean up—to prepare for the person to come in.

John the Baptist was kind of like a doorbell for Jesus. He let everyone know that Jesus was coming. John came first, giving everyone a chance to prepare their hearts for Jesus.

He invited people to confess their sins and be baptized, so that they could be clean when Jesus arrived.

Like John and the people he baptized, we can prepare for Jesus to come. We can confess and repent of our sins. We can ask God to make us clean. We can make our hearts ready to receive Jesus at Christmas!

WONDER: What do you do before someone comes to your house? How can you, like John the Baptist, be like a doorbell for Jesus?

> **PRAY:** Lord, what parts of my heart are messy? Would you help me clean up and be ready for you to come? Amen.

READ: A SELECTION FROM LUKE 1:26–38

In the sixth month the angel Gabriel was sent by God to a town in Galilee called Nazareth, to a virgin engaged to a man whose name was Joseph, of the house of David. The virgin's name was Mary. And he came to her and said, "Greetings, favored one! The Lord is with you." But she was much perplexed by his words and pondered what sort of greeting this might be. The angel said to her, "Do not be afraid, Mary, for you have found favor with God. And now, you will conceive in your womb and bear a son, and you will name him Jesus. He will be great, and will be called the Son of the Most High, and the Lord God will give to him the throne of his ancestor David. He will reign over the house of Jacob forever, and of his kingdom there will be no end."

LISTEN: Ask your mom or dad what it's like to be a parent. They might mention that it's both wonderful and hard, and that lots of it is bittersweet. They think you're the coolest person ever. (Yup, even if you have siblings! Shh, don't tell.) They love seeing the person you're becoming. And every time you grow taller and more independent, they probably want to cry.

When Mary agreed to become Jesus's mom, she may not have realized all that she was signing up for. She was probably doing something really normal, like brushing her teeth, reading a book, or walking home from a friend's house.

But once that angel showed up, nothing was normal anymore! Now Mary would be Jesus's mom—the mom of the Son of God. Her life was going to change a whole lot. She was going to feel everything your parents feel, except maybe even more. Her son is definitely the coolest person ever, and she got to help raise him! She also had to watch him die, which is maybe the worst thing for a parent. But she also got to see him come back to life as the Savior of the whole world.

Thanks to Mary, nothing is "normal" for us anymore, either. We get to live in a world where God became a human being. God has chosen to save the world. Through Jesus, God is making all things new!

WONDER: How did Mary feel about becoming Jesus's mom? What's different about the world because she said yes?

PRAY: God, thanks for becoming a human being. Thanks for choosing to become one of us and for saving the world. Amen.

A SPECIAL REQUEST

DECEMBER 23

READ: A SELECTION FROM MATTHEW 1:18–25

Now the birth of Jesus the Messiah took place in this way. When his mother Mary had been engaged to Joseph, but before they lived together, she was found to be with child from the Holy Spirit. Her husband Joseph, being a righteous man and unwilling to expose her to public disgrace, planned to dismiss her quietly. But just when he had resolved to do this, an angel of the Lord appeared to him in a dream and said, "Joseph, son of David, do not be afraid to take Mary as your wife, for the child conceived in her is from the Holy Spirit. She will bear a son, and you are to name him Jesus, for he will save his people from their sins."

LISTEN: Joseph could have said, "No way! I'm not going to marry her anymore. Even though I love Mary, I want to have a normal life. I don't want to be the adoptive dad of the Son of God. That's weird. People will think *I'm* weird."

But he didn't.

Joseph said, "Yes, I'll marry her. I'll help raise the Son of God. I'll let people think I'm weird."

Joseph cared less about what other people thought and more about what God thought. He cared more about Mary and less about himself. And because of that, God gave him a pretty cool part in God's story. God used Joseph to raise Jesus. Joseph got to teach Jesus how to use a hammer and build a chair, how to read the Bible, and how to love other people. Joseph got to be Jesus's dad.

WONDER: What things did Jesus learn from Joseph? What can you learn from Joseph?

> **PRAY:** God, Joseph reminds me that you can use me in amazing ways when I let you. What part do you want me to play in your story? Amen.

A LONG JOURNEY

DECEMBER 24

READ: LUKE 2:1–5

In those days a decree went out from Emperor Augustus that all the world should be registered. This was the first registration and was taken while Quirinius was governor of Syria. All went to their own towns to be registered. Joseph also went from the town of Nazareth in Galilee to Judea, to the city of David called Bethlehem, because he was descended from the house and family of David. He went to be registered with Mary, to whom he was engaged and who was expecting a child.

LISTEN: We're almost there! We've traveled through so much of the Bible this Advent, and now we're almost to Bethlehem. Who are we traveling with?

We're traveling with Mary. Her pregnant belly is big and round, and she's ready to have the baby! She doesn't want to be pregnant anymore. She wants to hold Jesus in her arms. As we wait for Jesus to come again, we're like Mary. We can get antsy, impatient for him to come back and make everything right.

We're traveling with Joseph, too. He doesn't know what to expect. He's never been a dad before. He doesn't even know how to hold a baby! We're like Joseph because we don't know what to expect, either! We hope we've done enough to prepare for Jesus to come again. We hope we're ready.

Jesus, come soon! We're excited for you to be here with us forever. We don't want to wait any more.

WONDER: What will it be like when Jesus comes again?

> **PRAY:** Jesus, I'm excited for you to come again. Will you help me be ready? Amen.

A BIRTH ANNOUNCEMENT

DECEMBER 25

READ: A SELECTION FROM LUKE 2:6–21

While they were there, the time came for her to deliver her child. And she gave birth to her firstborn son and wrapped him in bands of cloth, and laid him in a manger, because there was no place for them in the inn.

In that region there were shepherds living in the fields, keeping watch over their flock by night. Then an angel of the Lord stood before them, and the glory of the Lord shone around them, and they were terrified. But the angel said to them, "Do not be afraid; for see—I am bringing you good news of great joy for all the people: to you is born this day in the city of David a Savior, who is the Messiah, the Lord." … So [the shepherds] went with haste and found Mary and Joseph, and the child lying in the manger. When they saw this, they made known what had been told them about this child; and all who heard it were amazed at what the shepherds told them.

LISTEN: Eep! Have you heard the good news? Jesus is born!

A new branch is finally sprouting from the stump of Jesse.

Mary is pondering it all. As she nurses little Jesus, she's thinking about what it means that he is here, ready to save the world.

The angels are proclaiming it. They come as a huge choir, singing about how amazing God is.

The shepherds are a part of it, too. God chooses to tell them first. The shepherds aren't fancy or important, but they're the first ones who get to meet Jesus.

And today, you get to be there with the shepherds. You get to hear the good news. You get to meet Jesus. You get to go tell other people about it. God has chosen you! He wants you to have a part in his story.

WONDER: Why did God choose to tell the shepherds about Jesus before anyone else?

> **PRAY:** Jesus, we're so glad you've come! Thank you for being born into our world. Thank you for loving us enough to come save us and live with us. Amen.

JESSE TREE SYMBOLS AND BIBLE READINGS

DECEMBER 1
Isaiah 11:1-2
Tree stump with branch

DECEMBER 2
Genesis 1:26-31
Adam and Eve

DECEMBER 3
Genesis 3
Snake and apple

DECEMBER 4
Genesis 6:11-14; 7:17-8:3; 9:8-13
Noah's Ark

DECEMBER 5
Genesis 12:1-7
Tent and camel

DECEMBER 6
Genesis 15:1-6
Starry sky

DECEMBER 7
Genesis 37:1-36
Joseph's coat of many colors

DECEMBER 8
Deuteronomy 5:1-22
Commandment tablets

DECEMBER 9
Joshua 2:1-21
Rope

DECEMBER 10
Ruth 2:1-4:6
Grain

DECEMBER 11
1 Samuel 16:1-15
Crown

DECEMBER 12
2 Samuel 5:1-5
Sheep or
shepherd's crook

DECEMBER 13
1 Kings 5:5; 1 Kings 6
Temple

DECEMBER 14
Esther 4
Scepter

DECEMBER 15
Isaiah 9:2-7
Sun

DECEMBER 16
Isaiah 11:6-8
Wolf and lamb

DECEMBER 17
Jonah 3:1-5
Whale

DECEMBER 18
Daniel 6
Lion

DECEMBER 19
Micah 5:1-5
City of Bethlehem

DECEMBER 20
Luke 1:5-25
Praying hands

DECEMBER 21
Matthew 3:1-6
Baptism shell

DECEMBER 22
Luke 1:26-38
Virgin Mary

DECEMBER 23
Matthew 1:18-25
Angel of the Lord

DECEMBER 24
Luke 2:1-5
Sandals

DECEMBER 25
Luke 2:6-21
Baby in manger

Made in the USA
Middletown, DE
06 December 2022

17107925R00035